BE AFFIRMED

To B. Danielle

Thank you so much
for always affirming me,
even if it was not your
intention to do so.
I said "I'm not a poet."
You said "you just read a poem."
Thank you. Always, Angel

Be Affirmed

Fade to Black

By Angel Shanese

Rebel Iris, LLC

BE AFFIRMED
(Fade To Black)

Angel Shanese

DEDICATION

This book is dedicated to Mae Pearl, otherwise known as Mommy. Pearlie Mae was my mother's real name but, just like in most Black households, that I know of, calling your mother by her birth name was unacceptable. Being who she raised me to be, I switched her names around. Instead of "don't call me by my name", she would say "don't call me that." It's something I did until the day she passed away.

I almost decided against a dedication, but I've spent more time trying to make her proud this year than I ever did while she was alive. This book is dedicated to the woman who gave me verbal permission to use my voice, be angry & defend myself. I was a very quiet child, and I am so grateful she took the time to teach me these very vital lessons. As I think back on 2020, I know she would not have been surprised at the riots, condemned the looting, or scolded me for the many tears I have shed for people I've never met. I appreciate her not scolding the empathy right out of me, because she was hard in a sense, and for not ever teaching me that empathy is a weakness, I thank her, even now, for teaching me that Black isn't synonymous with guilt. Mae Pearl is the first person I ever heard say Black is beautiful, and that is no lie. Nikki Giovanni was asked, by Charlamagne tha God, about her quote "Show me a woman not full of herself, and I'll show you a hungry person."

Her response was, "...The first thing you have to do, when you wake up in the morning as a Black woman, is look in the mirror and smile at yourself. Because all of your life, all of your mother's life, all of your grandmother's life, we've been told we were ugly, and we were black, and so the first thing you have to do is you have to train yourself. So... you wake up and smile in the mirror, you look at yourself and say girl you're alright, because if you don't do that, that may be the only smile you get..."

Thank you, Mommy. Thank you for smiling at me.

Love, Ān

FOREWORD

When I met Angel Shanese several years ago, I was drawn in by her personal story of loss and desire. After a 2,000-mile road trip, my intrigue grew into immense respect for Angel, as I learned more about her growing up on the Southside of Chicago, becoming a wife and mother, the loss of a child, and her own struggles with malady and infirmity.

The poems in this book draw upon Angel's personal conflicts and infatuations. The captivating and brutal truths of which she writes are her own story, but many readers will recognize her torment, yearnings, and aspirations akin to their own lascivious cravings. The fervency with which Angel Shanese writes comes from a sincere deep dive into her own psyche.

Over the years my respect for Angel has grown into an undying friendship. Speaking truth has bonded us. I am honored to call Angel my best friend.

BE AFFIRMED, Shanese's first published book, emotes a relentless searching for authenticity and fulfillment. I write this foreword because hers is a vital voice in guiding those conflicted with their own current circumstances to pursue the fulfillment of their most ardent desires, and to strive for personal authenticity, always.

Resin Rebel
Founder/Producer,
Cinema Systers Film Festival
Lifelong LGBTQ Activist

PREFACE

Admittedly, I initially balked at writing a preface, and I am still not sure why. It could be a number of reasons, for which I don't have time to fully explore, but the main reasons hardly ever change. Imposter syndrome, anxiety, and self-sabotage have managed to talk me out of doing so much. When you grow up in situations where tough love and religion are what is poured into you, talking about yourself is not considered a sign of humility.

This book has been a long time in the making. However, these poems were written in the last four years. As I sit, there is now a woman of color in the White House. After a presidency that started off attacking Mexicans, my mind began reeling. I began waking up, daily, wondering what children of color around the world were hearing as the news played in their homes. The person occupying the highest office in the country was using words to paint brown people in a negative light. I was furious at times, and I would write about that. However, words such as "empathy", "love", "friendship" etc... would be on my mind, until I wrote about them, in some way.

These poems are direct results of these epiphanies and hand-selected to ensure that some form of love is now poured into all of us who've endured the constant verbal abuse.

I wasn't sure what to name this book. The title was a place keeper. A reminder, of sorts, to not pour negativity into myself. When you get to be this big old age, sometimes you have to be your own mom. My mom, if she were living, would have told me to, "Have faith in yourself, Ān."

When all of the compiling was done, and it was time to come up with a title, it just made sense to also pour that into you. May something resonate with you. May you feel seen, loved, heard & affirmed. You, my love, are enough.

Do your thing. Make your mark and ride your wave.
Illinois, 2020.
The Author

BE AFFIRMED
(Fade To Black)

Gentle Rise

I hope that you don't have to hit the ground running today
That you have time to
meditate
chant
or pray
As I sit here and watch my candlelight dance
I humbly ask that you're provided the chance
to witness beauty
experience kindness
and perhaps
even the feeling of having the world
in the palm of your hands
"Gentle Rise"

You're Everything

Be gentle with yourself
I want to tell you
you really are the shit
Amazing
And that person in your head
unfortunately
refuses to acknowledge it
That person is no more than a mirage
That voice
epitome of self-sabotage
The things you've come to believe
drowning out love and affirmations you hear
but don't truly receive
You yourself have your attention 24/7
as to where I just stop by
I can drop endearing letters in your delivery box
or write it in the sky
The words can all be carefully chosen
with love
You still won't see
that you are everything
Bliss incarnate
as The Maker intended you to be
It all goes over your head
It doesn't matter what we say
You hear "I'm not worthy" or
"I can't do anything correctly"
and you leave that on loop all day
You tell you
that you're useless
deserving of nothing but the worst

Sometimes I wish we shared a bed
so you can hear my voice first
before you get all in your head

You Belong

You can be invited
yet feel out of place
Ever been uplifted
but feel as fragile as lace
You can be told countless time
you're so pretty
but any advances
no matter how seemingly sincere
always mimic pity
This is weighing on my mind
It's got my mind blinking "Fully Occupied" like a hotel sign
I may be all of those things
but it's playing out like I have intruded
and however big the party is
all I feel is secluded
My mind is reeling
projecting my doubtful thoughts onto this painted ceiling
The antagonist is left to mull over her future
with three daggers secured in her heart
even the finest of doctors can't suture
Uncertainty must show all over my face
So I remind myself
"You do belong in this space"

Receive Your Gifts

I made a plan
opened my hands
and trinkets began to fall in
I reached out in darkness
I didn't see
the abundance of
information & affirmation
readily available to me
I told some friends "send good energy my way"
It's all I needed to say
Get you a crew like that
They got on it right away
Whatever I need
it's already here
I've planted that seed
What I've asked for
I've already received
My job is to simply believe
As I've always been told
since before I could even stand on two feet
I often reiterate
for my own sake "What's for me is for me"

Step Into Your Purpose

She stepped into her purpose
First she shook the shit off of her feet
She started singing
"I'm not bringing any old shit with me"
She snapped her fingers
tossed tiny braids over her shoulders
loving how it felt when no powerful forces had ahold of
her
Letting her shapely hips sway freely
she sang
"They call it love, but do they really know me??
Doooo do doooo do... they really know me"
She twirled in a circle
she held her arms up & smiled
while keeping with the rhythm
she sang
"It doesn't really matter dark child.
This has been a long time coming, now just take a little
time
to enjoy it. If they truly care, when you hold your arms out
they'll still be there"
She dropped her arms,
and flipped her wrist,
continued singing again
"I'm not about to do this"
As she swayed both arms, back & forth, in the air
"I don't really care... nope. I don't really care.
No hurt, no harm, shall prosper here."
She basked in the purest of light
in her purpose
She soared to spectacular heights in her purpose.

Be Unapologetically You

If you see me out shopping with a glint in my eyes
upon further assessment you suddenly realize
ya girl is grabbing butternut squash
while wearing sexy fishnet thigh highs
Don't contemplate it
walk on by
It's just me
I rarely go for the modest approach
To be completely honest
I prefer nudity underneath my overcoat
On days you're feeling especially sheepish
averting your eyes
covering your teeth
That's a good day to skip every bit of me
I'm filled with raw emotions
exerting them unabashedly
My words akin to the first pew
My body the church
If my clothes offend
you aren't ready for my words
My creed shall remain "come as you are"
Speak your mind
Just watch your mouth
Don't take that freedom shit too far
Feel free to leave
Or stay
Follow the rules in my space
It is not my business
nor will it be my fault
if you can't handle what I say
So If you get disrespectful
I won't hesitate to put you in your place

I write about the passion
losing it
having it
How we abuse it
in all of the ways
Always on display
That's the blessing of being your true self
Saying what you need to say
My mind drifts back to the homeless being turned away
at the church's door
How as a child I saw that rejection as being unworthy
if you appeared to be poor
or goodness forbid
the holy ones condemned you as a whore
I'm the mother
of this sanctuary where I sit high on my pew &
perception is observed
recorded from my third eye view
The tithes
written confessions on that which bears my face
words so precious I enjoy the after taste
Words which live on the tongues of voyeurs
who've carefully studied this space
There you'll find me
naked & unapologetic
saying the things so many of us have been warned not to
say
WE MATTER

Righteous

Don't talk to me I need to get this out
There's nothing more important than this right now
Writing now
There is nothing pressing to talk about right now
Writing right now
I'm feeling unimaginable pain
Write now
Fear is on overdrive
I'm just living out here
when what I really want to do is thrive
You kick harder when I'm down
You helped keep my head above water
then exhaust yourself trying to make me drown
I smirk
take a deep breath
preparing to be pushed down again
Don't wipe my tears
you are not my fucking friend
Get your red hands off of my face
Keep your wicked ass energy out of my space
Leave me alone right now
Just let me...
write right now

Take Notice

I stopped at the edge
Full stop
And there's a metal gate there
For a second
I wondered about its apparent suspension
in mid air
But that does not matter
What matters is
it's the edge and a gate is there

The Gift of Goodbye

Let go out of exhaustion
Fatigue
A better understanding of what doesn't serve thee
Make room for retribution
apologies
and peace
Give more energy to wonderments
Love
and less anyone around you who's only looking to be ap-
peased
Do the work required to hold on
Life is short
although the process is long
Forgiveness is preached on a daily basis
Forgive but don't forget the beauty in stasis
The ebb & flow in all living systems
Creating balance and health within
Why shouldn't this balance also apply to our minds eye
Sweet release
because you've already tried
Now give yourself the gift of goodbye

Public Consumption

I want to explain it
but for the complexities
Don't lay our problems at the world's door
Are we different
Yes
Magical even
Of course
These are the things we project
Does it matter
Yes
Is there more to do
Yes
The process starts with whom we choose to protect
Can we admit that it's human to want to cocoon what you
love
Indeed
Blackness stays on the preservation list

Manifest
(Don't Forget, We ALL Matter)

Wishing I had a thousand hands
summoning a thousand minds
willing them to understand
Believing
with everything in me
this desperate land will once again bear trees
There are remnants of where life used to be
I call to the goddesses
"Let Pope be right, and hope does spring eternal. Let there
be light!"
Before I knew it
I was back in bed
repeating
chanting
reiterating in my head
Drifting
Fading
Believing what I've said
Energy
It's never dead

Empathy > Apathy

I see empathy, in bright red letters.
Probably because it's an emergency
It feels as if apathy is in season,
as if careless is what so many aspire to be
It hurts so bad to know my sister is in pain
& my heart aches in a thousand ways to know my brother's
face will never be seen again
I can't scroll past Black bodies lying dead in the street
and not wonder what their kids do to eat!
I don't get it, and yet I do
Enough of us just don't care

Hold On, Love

I was once there
in a cave so cold & so dark
where my blood became the ink I used to gently leave my
mark
I emerged, quite scathed, but I emerged & am glad to still
be here
That cave is still in existence
flooded with my tears
I'm not exactly sure what guided me back to my light
I just know that I never want to go there again
because that darkness preyed on my frights
From beginning to end
that darkness told me I was unlovable
No one could possibly understand
I'd always be alone
I didn't deserve any friends
I'm not sure I'll ever have the energy
to put up a fight like that again
If you're doing it
Still trying to "make it through"
I'd rather transfer that energy to you
I know you've heard this so many times before
I know
I get it
sometimes people "just say shit"
My concern for you & others lost in darkness
is simultaneously
sincere & legit
I want to say take your time
or sing you sweet nothings with the words
Including but not limited to "everything will be just fine"
I won't do that to you

because I know that won't always be true
Instead
the promise I'll make
is "one day the breaths will be easier to take"
One day, the breaths will be easier to take
Love Always, Angel

Empathy Sometimes Make You Angry

I live to make you mad
Especially if you put all your effort into making me sad
It saddens me to see my brothers & sisters dying in the
street
It saddens me to see my sisters struggling to put shoes on
their
kids' feet
As we make excuse for those who've played
judge
Juror
And executioner
With their children's' mommas and daddies
It saddens me when I look around and I don't see anyone
who looks anything like me
because they aren't sure if the space is safe enough for
them to just fucking be
It's sad as fuck that my kid doesn't know
No matter how well he acts
there'll be some places he just shouldn't go
It saddens me that mentally ill people are locked up instead of getting help
It saddens me that little kids are being kidnapped by our
government
while millionaires only think of themselves
It saddens me that this poem could go on for years
because seeing sick people is sad to me
and grieving mothers have me in tears
Am I abnormal
or
do you too
empathize with those in pain all around you

Why I Write

I once wrote from pain
with wounds so raw
They left my pillow stained
And I feared writing anything notable
Because I'd have to hurt like that again

Here I am living on the verge
ready to dive in
being made to resist the urge

Essentially what I'm doing is

I'm suppressing a deep desire to purge

I shake my head because of all the wasted time

Trying

And unsuccessfully too

using every other tool I had to maintain my mind

Before I knew it
I was knee deep again

Holding on to a rope
being dragged my pin

Hoping
Like a lost child
to be reigned back in
Lest I lose it and burst from within

**It's Not Just You
(Fade To Black)**

I faded into blackness
the blackest of Black
Sometimes it has to be like that

I need Black at my fingertips
Black at my back
I need Black tunneling through my ears
I need to see Black images, and not just from slave years

I need this so bad
The blackest of the Black
Like sitting between my granny's arthritic knees
as she put my hair in plats Black

Like take this
and you'd betta not say nothing Black
Or we'll both be in trouble
and that's that on that

I need my phone calls to be Black
Like "mmmhmm I just wanted to check on you
I'll call you back" Black

Black like the color of my last born
BLACK like sistahs with their fists raised
because we can do that while we mourn

Black like I don't know you but that's messed up
Black like the earth could be on fire but we're still cutting
up

Black like the music makes your hips sway and you don't
know   how to dance
Black like forget all of that
they've had their chance

I want to sit in the middle of the Black Sea

Letting the salt water float me to where I need to be

Round tabling about the mythologies
And acknowledging this fucking PTSD

Approaching this trauma on another level
that removes it from the shit people tend to shovel

We don't truly realize the weight of it all
We are humans who're watching our brothers and sisters
fall

It's so much, I can't tell the whole room

So I step deeper into the Blackness-

right past any light

I wave barely acknowledging the moon

I bow down instead
to give greetings to Oshun
thank you for welcoming me
allow me to make these offerings

we worship you with

melanated mantras

singing songs of praise

There's congregation in this blackness

My church of choice

And it will be
for all of my days –

Know Thyself

You hear me talk and think she doesn't like herself
because I refer to my blemishes
or point out that my hair came off the shelf

You see me smile and it confuses you
You refuse to believe my smile is true

How does she say "I have big lips" without feeling shame
because these lips say more about my ancestry than my
own damned name

I can say "I wear weave" and still feel pride
this weave protects my mane that grows towards the sky
And this make up hides my blemishes
in hues that match deep dark beautifully melanated fin-
ishes
Nothing I wear takes away from who I am
nothing you could ever say
can again make me feel that way

Folks have made "traditional beauty" a slur
but I'll tell you what I know
never mind the things I've heard

I know beauty isn't what they claim it once was
that pretty is as pretty does
No more being held hostage by what you may see
It's not my business what you think of me
This world is not the authority on what is or isn't beauty
She may see dark skin
and think it's ugly
he may see a fro and think it's just fuzzy

I see that she's gorgeous in her own way
that girl has a sexy sway
her smile will brighten up an entire day
I see ALL of her & her
I see ALL of her too ~

Boundaries Are Healthy
(For You)

My lane is very narrow, and my wheels are aligned just fine

If we are going to remain close

stay in your lane
leave me to mine

Cross it, and you'll surely change all of the rules
Trust me when I tell you
I've got all of the tools

And I'll use every last one, just to see you completely un-
done

Of course the first rule of this club is to "harm none"

As Daedalus warned Icarus, "don't fly too close to the sun"

I fought the shade
with my hands tied behind my back

Ask the trees

I won

You're Wonderfully Made

Trees o'
Like limbs
We stretch in fellowship
different branches
from different trees
All special in their own way
they nourish me
It doesn't matter if they want to
or do it inadvertently
What matters is I drink them in
Letting their lessons flow through thoroughly
without becoming greedy
With only the intentions of contributing from now until
later
I wish to grow taller
stronger
in my own right
I need to join limbs with them
inch closer through the night
May my leaves spread at the perfect time
Let the little ones bask in this glorious sunshine
We are shade
They're protectors
We are magic
And we are wonderfully made

Play, It's Okay

Let's paint in the brightest hues
scarlet reds
aqua blues
I want to hum until verses fall from our lips
dance
laugh
talk
and sip
I need to share space
I've a deep desire to spend time
touch on subjects that flow through both of our minds
as we pick flowers that cascade from windows covered in
vines
I want to know if your heart has ever been broken
If you've found the remedy
I want to hear you tell me how you've come
are you where you'd like to be
and if your life was a journey you traveled alone
Please tell me how far
What I'm asking for is candor
in telling me who you are
Your hopes and dreams
Tell me how it really is
Not how it all seems
Do you believe this overwhelming feeling is reserved for
just me
If it is
I need clarity
and some transparency
to be assured nothing is at risk
especially my heart
as I expose my vulnerabilities

No more superficialities

Would you like me to start

Be Inspired
(e nina jay)

Sometimes
we exchange words
But even comfortable silence is remarkable
Your existence is enough to penetrate me
making me extremely aware of this moment in time
I want to save my place
I make a side note in my mind
to appreciate when we share space
The words you fill me with
they're all intricately laced
Looped around my body
anchoring my entire soul
I hope the dark
masks the expressions on my face
Your words left me craving more
There are so many things I'd like to know
Where're you from
Did you travel by water or stars
How'd you come to use your words as swords
And a salve for your scars
Before you go
I'd like you to know
I appreciate how you express my soul

You Are Lovable

Don't pull me off the shelf just to put me on the floor
Don't pull on my heartstrings & leave me wanting more

Don't ask me for what you'd never ever give me
Stop stabbing me just to stitch me up
Don't leave me staring wantonly
as you play with your new tea cups
Steadily neglecting me repeatedly

You could just set me free
I know you think of me just as a toy
But there's somewhere I could be

There's a toy store on the corner
the owner is really nice
She speaks to me when we cross paths
She has even repaired me twice

She says she'll keep me
if we were to ever meet again
So I think of her often
as I sit here on the end

Since you prefer other toys over me
please send me back to my friend

Stay Close
(Strive For Balance)

When there's more ebbing than flowing
Balance starved
Mind going
Expecting change
While all the while knowing
It's small wins
Big fails
Strong winds
No sails
Heavenly moments
in hell's shell
Waiting on someone to tip life's scale

Find Your Happy Place

Music moves me
It sits me up on the bed
It rubs my legs with vibrations
Music kisses me on my head
Music reminded me
on many occasions
I'm not yet dead
Music once moved my feet, when I had no will to run
Music also rubbed me raw
allowing me to be redone
Now I'm lying here with eyes full of tears
I realized what I really need, in this moment,
is music in my ears

Sometimes Peace Resides In The Melodies
(Nina Simone)

Sing me the sweetest lullaby
Tell me how you'll always love me
and that you'll never leave
I don't care if it is truth
just for a second, I want to feel like I'm everything to you
Just for a second, I want to feel I mean as much to you
as you do to me
I'm asking you to lyrically lie
and make it sound sweet enough to lull me to sleep

Move With The Beat

Seemingly, they were always out of sync. They continued dancing to the beat of their own drums, but the rhythm, at some point, would leave them on one accord. Before realizing it, they eventually began singing the same tune

Tea For 1
(Self-Care Everyday)

Decaf nights
concocted with cures of old
Swirling hibiscus
bits of saffron
steeping beneath beautiful marigolds
Hints of wild sweet orange
wafting up my nose
I sip
appealing to all of my senses
gently it all flows downwards
adding warmth to my soul

Love Insomnia
(Reflect)

I can't sleep
I've got love on my mind
The feeling of it
The hurt left from it
Love suspends actual moments in time
It's relevance in all of the things that has come & gone
My reluctance to reap these seeds I've sown, for fear of the
fragility, even though the harvest is my own
Oh, how it's absence can make all of life seem amiss
Since first it was felt in a simple kiss

It's confounding in
its' fluidity
How it travels through vessels
consuming all of me
Invading my body's supposed impenetrable traps
taking leaps through my synaptic gaps

Will love land in pools in my eyes
Or delicately climb my limbs to stretch the length of my
spine
leaving warmth to trickle down my thighs

Lucid Dreams (Trust Your Ancestors)

I should cloak myself
doubt what is right
dance happily though its day and hide in the night
Stay ceilinged in fairy tales
they feel better
they pled of me
Never question the moon
or the weight of the sea
Its lasting effects on the frame
or my wellness
as the sea becomes wetter
Disregarding my spills
although they only occur because of spiel after spiel
of broken black diamonds
I maintain it
this frame
though I buckle at times
I apprise those Sangoma shaking metaphorical bones
sacrificing the appearance of sanity
bringing forth what said bones read
I defend what some know nothing of
Making claims after never dipping their toes in
They toss around terms like Wiccan but these skeletons
were anything but
they are my ancestors calling to me
erasing all modern deities
Awaking me
they guide me gently requiring no proof
because unlike god's presented me throughout life in this
shell
offering me depths beyond all heavens and all hells
They knew me before I was

I'm flesh from their flesh, disseminating blood from their
blood
They wake me from my sleep, demanding I seek all that I
am
Beckoning for me to see through the sea
Rewarding me with truth
of not just me but
We

It's Okay, Hide

It's funny when people try to read me
Is she sneaky
Her eyes are always slanted
I wonder if she see me
That's sex in her eyes
Girl you must be freaky

What if I just don't choose to be read
Or want to be known as that black girl who just came back
from the dead
I may not want you to see the secrets I hide
nor take any part of me when you decide to ride

I may be thinking about 1997,98, or 2004
or all the personalities that have served me
and were later destroyed
because I didn't require their armor any more

Maybe I choose not to be read
because the last place I want to be is in someone else's
head

Don't peer at me

As a matter of fact
tell them to close my casket when you hear I'm dead

You only want to know because you're nosy
You don't care about my well being
or have any plans at all to satisfy me

Kisses

In its purest form
a kiss can transform a heart
In its most passionate
it can increase its rate
When it's given in sadness
it can seal all fate
And when it's given in rage
someone can catch a case
How now do I describe
I need to kiss you while I stare into your eyes
how can I explain
I want to kiss you gently
whenever I see you in pain
I want to absorb every bit of it
to see you smile again

Your Voice Is Vital

I wrote it down
and erased it
Feeling compelled to jot down it's lengthy replacement
Is there really a need for me
to show them from whence I bleed
Never been one to pick the scabs from my knees
There's a definite lack of trust
But then I think of Rosa Parks sitting upright on the front
of that Montgomery bus
I am old enough to know what the truth will get us
There's a price Blactivists pay
If anyone amplifies what we have to say
The attempt to silence us has gone on forever
Knowing it doesn't stop
This won't get better
So I tell my truths
It doesn't matter how
About how broken my heart is
How my mind functions like a plough
Overturning all of the weeds and unlearning complacency
I'm sowing Black seeds now
Reminding young ones occupying this space I'm in
Some people are experts at aversion
They refuse to see our scars
Knee deep in their dirty history
While making disparaging comments about ours
Displaying irrational anger whenever it comes to us
Tone policing
Making a fuss
My nerve kicked in
And here we are

Daughter of the earth
Product of the stars
Called upon to tell these truths
Freed from the thoughts of how they taste to you

Worthy

I never think of the amount of people I touch
although I speak & move intentionally
I do think of those who've managed to touch & or move me
and how I still rely on them so heavily
Those words, hands & magnetic energies
Many long gone
but etched in my memory
On my skin
In my mind
In the things I see
In my actions
My choices
And the places I be
Memories that serve to remind me
I deserve communication
Life is constant alterations
Take off those rose-colored glasses
And witness the world's saturation
Rest isn't just for people who are on vacation
Wisdoms that asked to be written down
For future generations
Because they too need to understand
Sometimes mercy must come from thine own hand
Without these people I wouldn't be able to see
Sometimes my grace must come from me
I am worthy

~~~

... there is more from Angel Shanese to come.
Look for her other works published by Rebel Iris and others.

CPSIA information can be obtained
at www.ICGtesting.com
Printed in the USA
LVHW080344090521
686901LV00017B/983

9 781736 734513